Psych Horse Handicapping:

USING YOUR HEAD TO WIN BY A HEAD AND BE AHEAD

Dr. John H. Edgette

Psych Horse: *Using Your Head To Win By A Head And Be Ahead*
Dr. John H. Edgette

Copyright © 2021 Dr. John H. Edgette

This publication is not meant to provide financial or psychological advice. It is for educational or informational purposes only. Case examples are entirely fictional and any resemblance to an actual person is entirely coincidental.

First Printing: June 2021

Dr. John H. Edgette
P.O. Box 1271
Fairfield, Iowa
USA
1 917-806-1850
John@edgettetherapy.com

About the Author

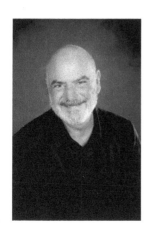

Dr. John H. Edgette (AKA "The Bettors Edge") is a retired clinical psychologist who was in private practice for over 30 years. He has lectured in over 30 states and 15 countries around the world. Dr. John has written over a half dozen articles for professional journals and has authored four other books. He now devotes his time to writing and being a professional "headicapper" while traveling the country in his motorhome with his Rottweiler Reno. His goal is to visit every race-track in the USA.

Other Books By
Dr. John H. Edgette

Winning The Mind Game: Hypnosis
and Sport Psychology

Hypnotic Erotic

Mating In The Wild : Fucking for Fun

Dedication:

To my Dad.......who taught me all about handicapping. I hope horseplayer heaven is all you
hoped it would be. When we buried you with
the next day's racing form, your off track betting
card, and your old bag cell phone we knew you
were going to win big. I just wish you had found
a way to give us your picks!

Table of Contents

Chapter One

Introduction:
Our Starting Gate

This book has been 50 years in the making. I'm just writing it now.

I still remember that cool June day when my father first took me to the track. I was 14. This book is the culmination of all the psychological knowledge I have acquired in the years since.

My dad was a 50's era dad who worked long hours in sales. Weekdays he worked long days and came home at 6:30 sharp where he would pour himself a drink, sit in his lazy boy chair, put his feet up, sip his scotch and read the New York Daily News. After singing "Some Day My Prince Will Come" my always angry mom put dinner on the table. Afterward, my dad would retreat back to the living room chair and continue to read his newspaper. Sometimes he would hide the racing form inside. Soon he would invariably fall asleep only to wake himself up with his own snoring and stumble off to bed having first gulped down the last slush of a third Dewars.

Saturdays were his day to mow the lawn and then pay the bills. He would station himself at a card table watching golf and sipping his first and second drink. Afterward, he would shower and pour on an excessive amount of Old Spice and then parade around like a peacock in his white boxers and crispy mom ironed T-shirt. It was only years later that I realised this pagentry was designed to attract the opposite sex in the hopes of mating.

Sunday's were wonderfully different. TRACK DAY! It was my dad's best way to escape my mom. And to avoid looking like a deadbeat, he soon learned that taking me along provided good parental camouflage for his weekly foray. He would give me $20 and circle the first, second and third favourites, reciting the percentage of each horse's chance of winning or being in the money. Of course, as is always the case, the gods of handicapping put the celestial fix in and I won big the first two times I went. I was forever hooked.

In the years after that my dad continued to teach me all the ins and outs of handicapping. His wisdom was supplemented by that of my brother who emphasised a whole different set of angles, as will be seen throughout this book. Then there were my cronies at the track, people you would never know if you did not occupy your favourite spot week after week. Characters like Scoobie, who illustrated the point of rewarding yourself for winning by yelling "THAT'S ME! Delmonico steak tonite!" every time he hit the triple. Then there was Big Dick Mick, whose sole quest seemed to be eating healthy at the track so as to stay focused throughout the card. " Great day for eating soup!!!" he would exclaim. Of course he never realised his quest…..most people at the track look like people at the track because of the food! The teachings of all of the people mentioned above were greatly supplemented by all my training as a doctor of psychology. This book is the result!

SO, DO YOU WANT TO IMPROVE YOUR HANDICAPPING?
BY:

- Adding a tool that may *increase your chances of winning!*

- Having a handicapping weapon that *works with any system* you already use!

- Adopting *a proven strategy* developed from the science of psychology!

- Using *a secret system* that no one has ever spoken about before!

- Implementing a method that is totally individualized and *remediates your gambling weaknesses while building on your strengths!*

READING THIS BOOK WILL ENABLE YOU TO ACCOMPLISH ALL THAT AND MORE!

NOW YOU ARE IN THE GATE, TURN THE PAGE AND YOU'RE OFF AND RUNNING!

Chapter Two

Knowing Your
Psychological Biases: A Test!

In this book I will introduce you to ideas that probably are new to you and will advance your handicapping. First off, we can help you discover what your counterproductive biases are. While we mainly are going to add psychological hacks to your handicapping, what follows are tendencies that you want to get rid of. The tendencies you discover are handicapping you! So DIAGNOSE AND SAY ADIOS!

Here's how!

First, handicap a card as you normally would using your usual bankroll. Of course, note your picks and how you are going to wager. Also note the amount you are going to bet on each horse and then put this off to the side.

Now get a new racing form and handicap the card again. This time, pretend you are betting with the same bankroll but for your best friend. Again, noting the amount and nature of all wagers.

Next, pretend you have what you would consider to be a massive bankroll where you are very wealthy. This being said, the pretend involves you being nonetheless very wise with your money. As before, handicap the card using another fresh form or computer print out. Continue to note the amount and type of bet as well as the horse or combination of horses.

Lastly, make believe you have a very very small bankroll and really don't want to lose everything. You want to be very cautious and bet smartly. Repeat the notations you made above.

Now is when everything comes together. Notice all the differences between the choices you made when you bet "normally" and the different scenarios. The differences will give you great clues as to where your psychological biases lie. For example…..

- Is your usual method of handicapping too wild and impulsive?
- Do you tend to bet too many favourites?
- Do you bet too many longshots?
- Are you in love with horses that have early speed?
- Do you bet too much early in the card?
- Do you play too many exotics?

Again, the differences you detect between your usual style of betting and when you were betting with a friend's money, when you were a rich man, and when you were poor and frugal all may show you the biases that hinder you from winning more at the track. You would also benefit from calculating which mock scenario wins you the most money. And if you want extra credit for this assignment, then repeat it two or three times. That way you will be sure to see highly reliable patterns to your biases and hence be able to correct them.

These are the kind of exercises that professional handicappers use to hone their skills. It takes work but no one ever said this would be easy. And it sure is nice to win more money!

Chapter Three

Last To First

When you handicap a race, especially one with a large field, you can actually get weary of handicapping the race. You then get sloppy, miss crucial things, and often rush to get through it and on to the next race. It is then one time when horses with low post positions tend to get overbet and ones with outside post positions get underbet; all things considered equal. My brother calls this "handicapper's fatigue".

This syndrome reveals itself more and more as the card goes on and on. And it is even worse when you are playing two cards at once or two race tracks in sequence. By the time you get to the last race of the day, you might barely even look at the horses toward the end of the field where your eyes are too blurry to see. You are too quickly to put a line through the latter horses, but they could then become overlooked winners.

These tendencies are compounded when horses draw in off the also eligible list. Punters tend to think they are misfits and considered unwanted race stepchildren that don't belong. Sometimes, handicapping fatigue is so bad that the bettor doesn't even know the horses have drawn into the race! Again, these could be your winners and they can win at a remarkably good price because others have skimmed past them too.

The situation is also worsened if you pick the horses you like and think can win early in the handicapping of a race. You then feel that you have your choice or choices and *YOU DON'T WANT ANYTHING MESSING UP YOUR NEAT LITTLE PLAN!* But that is no way to play the ponies. At least not play them smartly.

So if it is late in the day, you have large fields, horses are drawing in off the AE list and horses 1 and 3 look good to you....you have a perfect storm, the superfecta of sloppiness where maybe you can have a losing day to boot.

Luckily, doctors have found a cure for the disease of handicapping fatigue. Well at least this doctor has! The remedy is called "last to first". It is super simple and goes like this….. you handicap each race in reverse order; the last horse entered in a race to the first. This will compensate for your natural tendency to prefer low numbered horses over high numbered horses. That preference will be offset by handicapping fatigue and impatiens setting in as you encounter those horses of interest. And if it is early in the day and you don't yet know what the scratches are and who drew in from the AE list, then evaluate all the horses, out to #16 if need be.

Ok, so remember…. **GO LAST TO FIRST!**

Chapter Four

The Cardinal Sins of Handicapping: Avoiding Gambler Hell!

There are three major psychological and behavioural attitudes or orientations that can quickly send the gambol on the fast lane to being broke.

The first of these is that GREED IS THE DOWN-FALL OF THE GAMBLER. This sin is committed when a handicapper wins and then bets it all back and then some in an effort to hit ever larger jackpots. Folly! Learn to be satisfied with whatever your usual betting strategy allows! If you are guilty of this sin, repent now or be damned to a lifetime of picking up tossed tickets from the ground searching for the mistakenly discarded winner. That is one iteration of handicapper hell.

I once had a patient who went to gambler hell (Gamblers Anonymous, or GA in this case). One Christmas Eve, he went to the casinos for his favourite activity, the slots. He had a large credit line and used it; thirty thousand. He was down to the last thousand when he hit for 100k!!! Now what did he do? Cash out and buy his family and himself great Xmas presents on the way home? Save it to fund future casino trips, playing with *their* money? You guessed it. Nope. He wanted to win more and more. He had visions of being the next coming of Elon Musk. He had the machines figured out, which ones were ready to win. What happened of course is that he lost it all back, INCLUDING THE ORIGINAL 30 GRAND! He called me from his car on the way home. The credit line he used was actually from a credit card. His wife would soon know. Christmas was going to be hell. I talked him out of jumping off the Benjamin Franklin bridge and into a GA meeting that night. At least that would not actually be hell but a purgatory out of which he could redeem himself.

The second cardinal sin of betting (one should avoid committing these sins when casino gambling and the stock market as well) is LOSING YOUR DISCIPLINE. You have a handicapping system. It is supplemented and supercharged by the advice in this book. Stick with it through thick and thin! When you are tired or frustrated, you may be tempted to break ranks and "go for it", picking your horses in a very different manner than usual. You are foregoing (nice word choice for a horse racing book eh?) your tried and true systems. Please don't sin in this way and if you have, confess and repent!

The third deadly sin (the Catholic encyclopaedia defines cardinal sins as being the same as the deadly sins, except of course in "real life" there are seven of those) is CHASING YOUR LOSSES. You commit this sin when you are losing and psychologically are pissed and very badly want your money back. You sin by betting more and more on ever more improbable longshots in an effort to leave the track ahead. You abandoned your time honored system that has served you very well in the past in favor of selling your soul to the parimutuel devil. Penance for this sin is committing to being faithful to your regular handicapping method supplemented by the psychological hacks espoused in this book.

SINNERS REPENT! So consider being REBORN AGAIN in the name of Secretariat and Mother Ruffian!

Chapter Five

Be Biased Against Confirmation Bias

O k, let's talk about confirmation (NOT *conformation)* bias. CB is a scientific principle that can be applied to life in general. It is well researched and can be applied to activities of everyday living ranging from playing the stock market to discerning which type of car breaks down most often. Simply put, CB states that when you hold a strong belief, you tend to notice and remember events that prove it true and forget those that disprove it.

So if you believe that people with red hair have fiery tempers, you will confirm this belief by noticing and remembering every time a redhead has a rage reaction to something and dismiss all the times they react to adversity with calm thoughtfulness. Their belief is thereby affirmed and confirmed.

If you think all Fords are prone to having transmission problems at around thirty thousand miles then you will perceive it in accordance with the principle of CB.

Equine dentistry? Happens there too! In the Middle Ages it was taught that horses had a certain number of teeth. This "fact" was believed and taught and of course frequently observed to be true. It was only centuries later that an equine dentist carefully counted a horse's teeth without bias only to discover that the number was different from what veterinary schools had taught. This is a case of what we could call "imaginative confirmation bias" wherein the "proof " that we are correct isn't even observed in actuality, but instead created in the mind.

In the superstitious world of gambling, CB runs rampant. Take craps for example. There is an age-old belief that "dice on the floor, devils at the door". This refers to the toss of the dice being errant such that it goes out of play and onto the casino carpet. The "devil" part of the myth refers to the belief that the next throw will turn up a seven, which most of the time means that most patrons lose.

Examples of confirmation bias abound in horse racing. For example, it is widely believed that breaking through the starting gate prior to a race is the "kiss of death" for a horse. All who believe this can remember every single time they had a bet on a horse and lost due to this misbehavior. None of these folks remember all the times their horse broke through the gate but won, having been eager to race.

Handicappers also over believe in some trainer patterns. Take my dad for example. He once had a 50-1 winner betting on a horse out of the small barn of a long time NY trainer, Nat Krone. Krone had claimed the horse, moved him way up in class and put him on the turf. Forevermore, every next after claim race a Nat Krone horse ran in was heavily bet on by family Edgette. This was before computer betting, simulcasting, and even off track betting, so we would all take off work and scurry to the track to get our money down. Well, we never saw a Nat K horse ever win the first race off claim ever again. My dad went to his grave with this confirmation bias, having actually had no repeat performances to confirm his personal myth! His one big win was enough to rigidly lock him into this counterproductive betting strategy. It was as if he had anticipatory CB, always certain that confirmation was but one race away. It was good that my brother Tom and I never saw a Krone horse win post claim or else we too would be taking this lore to the grave!

Chapter Six

Myths Make Money, But Not In the Way You Think

A myth is an inaccurate idea that people cling too religiously. They abound in horse handicapping and because of that, you can bet contrary to them winning via "headicapping". That's right, if you don't buy into a false horse belief you are going to get better value. Psychologically, people who believe in a certain myth overbet horses based on it. If you bet in the other direction you can make money off of other peoples erroneous psychological belief system.

In this chapter we will examine three common myths that plague handicapping. The first has to do with weight. Back in the late 60's when I first started betting the ponies, it was common to read in the paper such things as "*picks up two pounds since his last race*" and " *drops three pounds and figures to be closer*"

A decade or more later, this thinking dropped off. Why? Because, a couple of pounds here or there on a 1,300 pound beast doesn't mean anything. Nada. Zip. Nothing. Yet in some quarters, this belief lingers and you can put that to work for you.

So to capitalize on this psychological flaw that some still entertain, consider betting the opposite way. So if the press is warning you off a horse because he "has never won carrying today's weight", give him a second look because the value is better then it would be otherwise. In a similar way, if TV analysts/experts like a horse because he is dropping weight, consider another pick. These are not absolute deal breakers or makers, just handicapping considerations.

If anyone still has doubts that weight does not make a difference, consider that in hurdle races where horses carry significantly MORE weight. And they not only have to run fast but JUMP too!

The second and third myths have to do with cross cultural psychological expectations that are held to be true in the U.S.A but are known to be bogus to those racing abroad. One holds that fillies and mares should not compete against horses, colts, and geldings. Here we make such a big deal about this that betting on any female daring to do this is front page sport section news. Horses such as Racheal Alexander and Swiss Skydiver become fan favourites while the big money goes in another direction. Hence, bet on the girls as they represent better value. And winning money isn't necessarily about picking lots and lots of winners, but rather consistently getting a better than expected return on investment.

In North America it is considered a big, big negative for a horse to ship anywhere to race. Shipping out of town is held against a horse at the betting windows. Shipping across country means that that horse will go off at much longer odds then it "should". Shipping abroad is generally considered such a kiss of death that owners, trainers, and others wonder whether the horse will ever be the same again! However, they all do relatively well and vanning or flying far seldom has a negative effect on a horse's career. Doubt this? Well, note that in Europe horses regularly fly to and from Great Britain and win, win, and win. They also fly across the pond to North America and do likewise. So it is wise to seriously consider these selections when they come to North America. There is great value due to the prejudice against them. Remember…..the wise win.

Chapter Seven

The Psychology of
Betting First Time Starters

O k, I'll get to the point right away. DO NOT BET FIRST TIME STARTERS ENTERED IN MAIDEN CLAIMING RACES FOR UNDER $50K. This is because every trainer, and especially the owners, want to believe that their new two year old may be the second coming of Secretariat. They want to give their purchase a chance to do good by them and so any horse half decent will be given a shot or two at Maiden Special Weight races. And then they will drop down to maiden claiming races. That is logical and they sure can be bet if it looks like they can run a bit but would appreciate the class relief. Nonetheless, do stay away from horses on that drop down that look like total dogs, having perhaps finished 17 lengths behind the winner or being pulled up in their MSW efforts. Again however, any horse running in a maiden claimer as a first time starter has been given up on and you should find a betting alternative. That is some of the psychology of where people enter their bright and shiny new horse.

That said, there are a couple of exceptions. First, there are a few trainers who wisely place their horses where they can win. If they worry they will get claimed, they are perhaps prepared to just take purse money and run or maybe they have bet a few mortgage payments on their "good thing" and will do well no matter what the outcome. In any event, know these trainers from their history of placing their horses this way. You can find those statistics online but most easily in the past performances published by Brisbane (available free when you use the TwinSpires racing platform which can be accessed through a free app).

A second exception is a trainer who historically likes to give even his or her good horses an easy and confidence building first start. A prime example of this is Christof(sp) Clement. He occasionally enters his potentially top horses in even $40k maiden claiming races. This not only gives them an easy first start, but also allows them to qualify for optional claiming allowances for horses who have started for that claiming price or lower. That is a safer place for a valued horse to be entered as they can run without being offered for purchase and against easier company.

In summary, unless one of the above exceptions is in play, steer clear of horses entered for the first time for a tag below $50k.

Chapter Eight

Changing Positions

You don't have to be a horse whisperer to know enough about horse psychology in order to improve your betting strategies. There are certain things that if you attend to them, will make you more successful at the betting window. If you mind the horse's mind, even a bit, you are likely to win more.

Psychologically, horses don't like to be trampled. I mean really, who would? What this means is that when a horse has a far outside post it will instinctively move away from the pack. So when you see a head on shot of the start of a race, you invariably see the horse in the 8,10, or 12 hole veer out toward open daylight, in any race, any place, and at any level. What this means is that that horse will need to be 3-4 lengths better than the rest of the field to win. Couple this with the fact that it is starting a number of yards away from the rail anyway and you have a horse that will need to be 5 lengths better than the rest to get the victory. This problem is compounded if the race starts on or near a turn. There, of course, more lengths are lost breaking from the outside. Unless the odds are outlandishly good or the horse is going to make a beeline straight for the lead, it is best to avoid betting the outside horse.

A related but less serious issue occurs when a horse draws the inside post. Then, it is common for horses to break inward, again away from the pack. This is somewhat less serious because there are fewer lengths to lose but the horse will likely lose position and may even need to take back. This predilection is even more pronounced in 2 year olds and first thing starters. Moreover, this issue is further compounded if the race is coming out of a chute. That wide open expanse to the left of the one hole may appear very tempting to the point where the horse may have to fight its way back onto the main track. It sometimes can be so serious that a runner will brush the rail or even crash or jump it! I only recommend betting the 1 horse if the odds are good, the horse is seasoned, or it is going to jet to the front. Speed from the rail will always be king in my opinion.

Horses are herd animals. Psychologically, they do not like to be alone. This is such a strong tendency that when a horse is boarded and put out in a field alone it will have something akin to a panic attack. The owner will need to get an aged equine "babysitter" to keep it company. Sometimes even a goat will suffice! In any event, being herd animals and hating to be alone explains why some horses hang or even pull themselves up once they make the lead. They want to be with the rest of the fold. Under those circumstances, a wise trainer will instruct a jockey to wait for the very last moment to take the lead in a race. If the connections know to do this, the horse is a fine bet but if they don't, then the horse will forever be likely to flatten out and wait for his buddies to catch up.

The above explains why some horses have seconditis, or even thirditis. They don't want to leave the pack to win or they dare not beat an alpha horse. Or sometimes both. They make excellent triple or exacta plays as long as you don't play them on top. The syndrome I describe is perhaps best illustrated by that legendary horse from the 70's, Jacques Who. An almost ghostlike grey, or a rare white, he notoriously could be counted on to finish second. He made playing exactas very easy.

Psychologically, horses are creatures of habit and it is really hard to break them of their habits. Horses who have gate problems (hesitating, hitting the gate, slamming other horses) will tend to continue in that way to the detriment of your wallet if you do not heed this advice. It is even problematic to be in the slot next to one of these trouble prone types. They are likely to slam into you and compromise your chances. Nowhere are handicappers more aware of this then when betting greyhound races. There, in the program, which serves as the form as well, they often have arrows indicating the habitual way a dog breaks. If the dog to your right and left tend to break away from you then it is clear sailing. If they both tend to break into you then you are likely in for trouble. Knowing these dog preferences is even more important than in horse racing because dogs do not have astute jockeys keeping a firm hold of the reigns on the opposite side to which the horse will want to go.

Horses are acutely aware of status. That is, there are alphas and there are zetas and everything in between. This is why a drop in class helps so very many horses win. Figuratively speaking, and psychologically speaking, they look around and with confidence say "I've got this". Drop downs are good bets if it seems as if a horse could use a confidence boost.

The overarching point of this chapter is that psychologically, horses are herd animals with strong instincts that quickly become habits. Additionally, to paraphrase the legendary show jumping trainer George Morris, horses need to have the right balance between bravery and fear. They have a curious plethora of both. Too much fear and they will have anxiety that will over-ride the will to win. Too much bravery and they will shoot to the lead, burn themselves out early, and inevitably fade.

Chapter Nine

What's In A Name?
Value? Or Not?

On Wednesday January 13th, 2021, the 9th race on a rather mediocre card at Gulfstream Park featured two horses with similar stats. I deemed that either could win so I bet both for different dollar amounts so that whichever one won, I would make a good amount of profit.

One horse's name was Hercules and the other was named Turkey Freeze.

I bet both but which was the better value? All things equal, which horse would you bet if you could only pick one? Most would say Hercules because it is a strong and powerful name, unlike the other whose name is lame and goofy. Hercules wound up going off as the favourite and Turkey Freeze the third choice.

Though they had similar capabilities, and hence each a chance of winning, Turkey Freeze was the far better value. Why? It was because his odds were longer even though he could have as easily won. And why was he longer odds? Surely because of his name, especially compared to his adversary.

Horses with weak and odd names go off at longer odds then they "should". A 15-1 shot who goes off at 50-1 because his name is "Poop" is a much better value then a horse named "Sure Winner" who is 6-5 but should be 2-1. Yes, we want to bet the horse that will finish first but in the long run we will do better seeking value. The risk/reward ratio shifts in our favor. Such is the psychology of names.

These opportunities show up all the time. On an earlier card in December at the same track, two horses with the worst names ever ran in different races. One was named Freezer Burn (no relation!) and the other Perspiration! I thought it was a misprint or a joke! Who named these horses? Did they really expect that one day at the Kentucky Derby they would hear "AND DOWN THE STRETCH THEY COME! IT'S GOING TO BE FREEZER BURN TO WIN BY AN ICICLE OVER PERSPIRATION!"? But all kidding aside, darned if that exacta wouldn't have paid big!

As mentioned above, the reverse can be true and horses can be overbet. I have a fun example of that from Aqueduct in the 70's. Two horses were coming down the stretch neck and neck on an ironically frigid winter inner dirt track day. Their names? Nudie and Dare to Be Topless! Although those names are not Triple Crown material by any means, they nonetheless probably were over-bet due to how fun and unusual their names were.

Well, such is the mental side of horse names. None of the above should either determine who you do or don't bet on. These points are just something to keep in mind when you are making your handicapping decisions.

Chapter Ten

Women Love Silk(s)

At the few tracks that attract tourists, and particularly women tourists, certain factors unrelated to performance can influence odds, and hence your return on investment. Knowing what these are and how to use them to your betting advantage is instrumental in coming out ahead at the end of a day, or year.

One of these factors is the color of a horse, believe it or not. Greys are always somewhat overbet but even more so at touristy tracks where many people are there mainly for fun. Scientific research has shown that this holds less true for roan horses (mixture of grey and brown hairs, found on young horses destined to be fully grey) but MORE true for the rare fully white horses. Take for example the infamous 70's cult favourite "Jacques Who", who was known for three things; being pure white, being terribly overbet, and consistently finishing second. In a similar vein but to a lesser extent, the rare black horse gets overbet. To a lesser extent though because it is less noticeable and less outstanding. The exact extent to which it gets overbet is mitigated by other aesthetics such as whether it is a sole white "sock" or four matching white socks. The point here is that you should lean toward the commoner when picking your winners.

Then there is the color of the horse's silks. At female fan favourite touristy places like Saratoga, Del Mar, and Royal Ascot, how attractive a horse's silks are has an influence on the price the horse will pay. Likewise for ugly or even nondescript silks. The worst nondescript silks are the ones that are given out when a horse ships into a big time track from a track that does not allow individual barn colours, mandating jockeys wear monochrome silks that match their saddlecloth. These horses then stand out in a negative way at the big league track by being assigned the generic track silks. At Aqueduct, for example, those are a uniform teal color with a huge "A" on the back. Sometimes there are even a couple of horses in a race given such informative wear. Informative? Yes, they might as well have a huge sign taped on them "small track, small time ".. In any event, the point here is that to bet wisely, players best shy away from the horse with the pretty silks but give EXTRA consideration to those small town horses with the generic silks, as they are often talented but under bet. Bettors may know what silks a horse's jockey is wearing but horses don't!

Now, onto names again. Elsewhere we have discussed how horses with goofy names like "Crumb Bun" (just glanced at today's Gulfstream card and yup, he's running!) are frequently under bet and thus represent good value. But what about the opposite? Well yes, horses with power names can be overbet. For example, a horse I once owned a share of, Phone the King, probably took a tad more action then he deserved. Had Man of War and Ruffian come back from horse heaven, it would not only be their reputation that would result in them being overplayed but their strong names as well.

Yet it is not just power names that attract the wagering dollar, it is horses that have a name someone identifies with. These names do not unduly move the overall action but may sway a particular individual in a counterproductive direction. For instance, a horse named Tom's Take may not be overbet by the general public but is likely to bias every Tom around to bet on it.

This would include my brother Tom, who has a bad habit of betting big on any horse that has Tom in its name, even if it is Thomasina. The point here is that as an individual bettor, don't play or overplay a horse for sentimental reasons. So if you happen to have six cats, don't become overly enamoured to an entry named Kittens Galore.

In summary, whether we take into consideration horse color, silk color, power names, or personal name preferences, we need to counteract both fan and one's own bias in service of not only being objective, but winning as well.

Chapter Eleven

Claim This Knowledge

Would you claim a horse for thirty thousand dollars only to run him for $10k? After 6 months on the shelf? After 3 dud performances? Just to win for once? There is a psychology to the claim box that it is good to sync up with if you want to win. Ignore it at risk to your wallet!

That thirty thousand dollar horse, assuming you are not a huge operation, is a very valuable commodity that you have high hopes for. Make some changes in running style, equipment, or training regime and win allowance races? Enter restricted stakes and have a shot? Ship to the state the horse was bred in and find a much easier company (currently living a stone's throw from Canterbury Downs, I realise just how many Minnisota bred horses there are!). Aspire to win an out of town ungraded stakes? Ship your mare around looking to garner some Grade 3 black type to ensure her value as a broodmare? Lose the horse via a claim for $62.5k and double your money? Sure! Any or all of the above!

Note that none of the above scenarios involves dumping your prized possession into a cheap claimer. That pretty much only happens if you have given up on the horse because he is no good. So if you see this taking place in the racing form, do not bet this horse. In fact, since it could be dropping down so low it could beat anything and could win, skip the race entirely and consider it one of those racetrack unknowns. If you are playing pick 4's, 5's and 6's, then use the horse because once again, it may win but go a little deeper in that race, use at least 2 other horses.

There are exceptions to the above strategy. One is when a barn is trying to unload a decent but not excellent horse because perhaps they have so many other horses. For example, on the New York circuit at present, the powerful and huge Klaravich stable seems to want stakes horses only such that fairly good allowance horses get significantly dropped down in the claiming ranks. These horses can certainly win as they are not being dropped down because they are hurt or otherwise damaged goods.

Another exception occurs when a horse was purchased or claimed at a low price and ran for a way higher tag for a bit and now returns to a level somewhere around where he was claimed. That horse is not being dumped but rather he has simply accomplished his mission and returns "home".

The last exception is rare but does happen. Sometimes a trainer or an owner wants to win the title at a short meet and be king of that track. It is prestigious and earns you accolades and/or more horses in your barn. So, in the final days of a meet you see horses drop to a winning level to accomplish the above. You typically see this every year at Saratoga, most notably in recent years with the rivalry being between Todd Pleacher and Chad Brown, both outstanding trainers.

If none of the above exceptions apply, avoid betting the horse in question. You will save yourself a losing ticket. Winning not only involves picking winners, it also entails avoiding losers and false favourites. And as you have seen, much of that can be accomplished by utilising the principles of psych-handicapping.

Chapter Twelve

Training Your Psyche With Trainer Psychology

Owners and trainers are smart people. They want to win. They want to make money. They want nice horses.

In terms of winning and making money, if you had a horse who had won a race handily, what would you do? You would no doubt run him back as soon as possible against tougher company for a higher purse. Right?

So then why would you, as a trainer or an owner, rest your horse for months on end after a nice victory. Most likely BECAUSE THE HORSE IS HURT. Don't bet these horses. If there is a bullet work or some other indication that the horse may come back fit and ready, include him in your exotic wagers or pass the race but do not bet him straight. That is not a good value.

There are two other indicators that the horse may be ready to roll off a layoff. One would be if the trainer has a strong history of winning with fresh horses. The other would be if the horse is of elite caliber and the connections wanted to freshen the horse for much bigger and better things to come. Other than these exceptions, pass, pass, pass.

In terms of wanting nice horses and making money, consider what it means when a trainer/owner combo claims a horse back. It means they know the horse, like the horse, and want it back in their stable. It is quite a complement and quite flattering to the horse in question! Be sure to seriously consider betting these horses. You would be well advised to bet even more if the horse has been claimed back twice, claimed back at a higher tag then it was lost for, or claimed back right after it was lost.

By synching up with owner and trainer psychology in these and other ways, you are using your head to get into their head and get ahead.

Chapter Thirteen

It Is Not Telepathy: Horses Know How Handlers Are Feeling

Thoroughbred racehorses can sense how their handlers are feeling. This is not a "New Age" kooky idea nor is it a matter of mind reading, telepathy, or thought control. The communication mainly takes place through muscle to muscle sensing.

This is where psychology comes in. The emotions a jockey feels will be subtly transmitted to the horse the second he or she is given a leg up into the saddle. Thoroughbreds are exquisitely sensitive to every muscle twitch. A confident jock will instill confidence in his horse. A slumping, depressed, nervous, or divorcing jockey will convey certain feelings to his mount, yet, the horse won't know exactly how to interpret this. It knows nothing of the heartbreak of divorce. He is going to think something bad is about to happen in the upcoming race.

Your solution then is to get as much inside information around the track as possible. It is good to not only know who is down and out but who is head over heels in love or who is basking in the glow of having a lovely newborn child.

Thankfully however, you don't just have to rely on insider info to use this tip. Informally monitor what you can objectively see and know about the jockey. Is he or she basking in the glow of just winning an Eclipse Award or are they coming back after a horrible fall and likely terrified to split horses to win in deep stretch?

What is the jockey's mind set and work ethic in general? Is this a hot young up and coming jockey who will give his all no matter who is the mount? Or is it a tired veteran jockey who is resentful that his agent put him up on a 60-1 shot who has not finished within 12 lengths of the winner in his last 10 starts in $4k claimers.

Nothing illustrates the effect of the psychology of the jockey on the performance of the horse better than the saga of Steve Cauthen. Right from the start of his career in the 70's he was on fire, often winning 3 or 4 or even 5 races on a nine race New York card (yes, that's how old I am, we only had 9 race cards back then). He could get up on a mule and win by 5 lengths. Then something happened. He went on a long, long losing streak. He could not buy a winner. Fans went from having to bet Cauthen in each race to betting anything but him. It was painful to witness. All of a sudden he could not buy a winner.

I am not sure what happened and I am not sure anyone else does either (thankfully his luck did change eventually with the advent of a geographical cure - he went to Europe and rode and later trained for the Queen). What happened and why is not the point however. The point is that one can be sure that to some extent, his mind set on the way up as well as the way down influenced his horses. Just how much we will never know.

The lesson here is to monitor jockey mind sets to every extent possible. Notice who is upbeat and laughing jovially in the walking ring and who looks dour and hung over. This and all else you can garner. YOUR gambling mindset and hence your psychological and financial success depends on it!

Chapter Fourteen

Keep Your Mind on Your Money And Your Money On Your Mind: Part One

Books on handicapping are full of advice as to how much you should bet on a given horse and how. Or how much and when. None however, speak about the CURRENCY you bet with, what you do with WINNINGS, or the best ways to DEVELOP A BANKROLL. These issues are surprisingly psychological.

Let's start with bankroll development. For peace of mind, so you do not worry about taking money out of your kids mouths or depriving your family of heat, find a way to fund your hobby that is acceptable to you and yours. I say "hobby" because developing funds and dealing with money is a whole different ball game for the professional gambler. Dealing with that is far beyond the scope of this book. The recreational gambler primarily needs a guilt free way to have betting money in order to be psychologically free to win. Shame, guilt, and sneaking around hampers the psyche such that judgement is impaired and the fun of wagering is lost.

Here are some examples of creative ways to garner gambling dollars. Sam funds his twice monthly trips to the track by taking an extra $60 out of the ATM every time he withdraws money.

He puts it in a special envelope in a secure place at home so that it does not just dissipate from his wallet for everyday needs. This method means he will not need to scrounge up the money to bet come track day.

Prasid takes his annual bonus from work, "found money" to him and his family, and it becomes his annual bankroll for his forays to the track. When it dries up, so do his ventures out to the local race book.

Lionel does likewise with his quarterly commission checks. His base pay is so high and he works so hard, both he and his wife agree his track time and the money spent constitute warranted stress relief. Shame free, guilt free, and maritally sanctioned.

My brother Tom, a consummate handicapper mentioned elsewhere, lives in Saratoga. You don't live in Saratoga without betting the ponies. Not that he wouldn't otherwise! Anyway, a very successful businessman, he nonetheless has a side hustle leading spin classes at the local Y. It keeps him fit as he helps others stay fit and he makes a bit of "found" money each month. He has this directly deposited into a designated bank account. He does not touch that money all year until the start of the meet in mid July. Then those are the funds he uses throughout the six weeks of racing. Guilt free, shame free, and getting the good housekeeping seal of approval!

These are some examples of responsible ways to fund recreational horse betting. In the next chapters we will explore the optimal way to bet and the optimal physical way to interface with your funds. We will also explore the never before addressed topic of what you do with all your winnings!

Chapter Fifteen

Keep Your Mind On Your Money And Your Money On Your Mind: Part Two

With what do you bet? Yeah, gotcha, you say "money". But how do you experience and interact with money? Ok, so now you think I've gone mystical/ philosophical on you? New agey even? Not so, and now you will see why. It is VERY psychological.

Some people bet with green bills, going up to the tellers windows. Some people call in their bets via "phonebet" or some such. Most these days do it via computer remotely or even on site. Which way is best? "All the same" you say, "money is money". Not so!

Bet with the actual green bills, at a teller window, if at all possible. Avoid the temptation to get a voucher and bet via track machine. Yes, I am telling you it is best to stand in line, wait, and then reach into your pocket, grab your wallet, pull out a Jefferson or Benjamin, and orally speak your bet. Then you get to check your tickets, put them in your lucky pocket, and go back to your seat. Again, why?

Because it is tangible. You can touch the money, touch the tickets, and interface with a real human being. Heck, I would have you bet with gold nuggets if I could! This way, your bet is more real. It is better thought out, less impulsive, more intentional, and you are more likely to bet just the correct amount. You will value your winnings more and see the textured dollars go right into that wallet of yours.

Handling things in the other ways makes you vulnerable to spending too much, in a cavalier fashion, and not appropriately appreciating your bet and your winnings, or losses. This is why credit cards are freely issued, online shopping is encouraged, and casinos make you bet with chips. That way they know you will spend more and more impulsively. Can you imagine how different things would be if when playing craps or blackjack you had your bills out and each time you bet you had to take one or more and put it on the table? And then when you were up a thousand, imagine how much more likely you would be to walk with the winnings rather than keep betting and lose it?

Now I hear you saying that you can not go to the track that you are playing that particular day. As

I write this, I am in frigid Philadelphia waiting to reward myself for writing this chapter by playing the Santa Anita card later. So I get it. Hence I have developed a system for dealing with the intangible action of pressing a few keys on my computer to gamble. Making things touchable/ tangible. Finite. Concrete. Real or realer.

In this system I have my days bankroll, in cash money green, and next to my computer. Every time I place an internet bet I take the "real" money from the bankroll pile and put it into a live bet pile. If I lose, it then transfers to a loss pile. If I win, I take the winning out of a special cashier pile I have set up and put it into a winnings pile.

I do not put the winnings into my daily bankroll pile. That would be a formula for surely betting more than I intended for the day and perhaps losing it all back. Also, to combine winnings with bankroll means that I won't properly appreciate what I have won! Those winnings need some love, attention, and appreciation! It is very psychological. By intermittently putting a focus on your winnings, you are telling your subconscious mind in a subliminal way that this is what you want more of. It is the law of attraction. Trust me on this! Remember, I am both a psychologist and hypnotist!

Ok, so those are my recommendations for how to bet and what to bet. In the next chapter you will find suggestions as to what to do with those winnings, and how that can in turn influence how much more you win! Again, It's all very psychological.

Chapter Sixteen

Keep Your Mind On Your Money And Your Money On Your Mind: Part Three

In this chapter we will discuss what to do with your winnings. No book on handicapping has ever addressed this issue!

Most recreational gamblers, when asked what they do with their winnings, would say "I spend them!", while looking at me with annoyance. But while bettors do spend their profit, they do not spend it wisely. Winning, spent right, encourages your subconscious mind to subtlety but powerfully orient toward accruing more winnings. This is not New Age fluff but a research proven psychological fact called the "Law of Attraction". On the other hand, winnings spent semi-randomly gives the subconscious mind the message that winning is pointless because you are using your profit to do what you would do with money gotten from any source. That demoralises the mind and indirectly, the person as a whole.

Frankly put, the vast majority of bettors take their winnings and put them in their wallet and spend it on paying bills or even everyday items as if it were a routine ATM withdrawal. The next most common thing is for gamblers to use their winnings to gamble more, eventually and inevitably losing it all back to the track.

What then is the wise thing to do? Well first off, have a dedicated section of your wallet or a seperate pocket for your bankroll. Do not under any circumstances combine it with your everyday money.

Next, have a special wallet section or pocket for all bets that you cash, including the dollars you wagered to get the win. This way you will not commingle winnings or even capital invested with your bankroll. And because you are putting all the money you got for a winning ticket in that separate place, your bankroll will remain strictly the money you have to bet that day. It will not be corrupted by money that has already been invested and is being recycled. So that special wallet section or pocket will actually be not just for winnings, but for money invested to obtain those winnings as well.

You leave the track a winner. Do you buy groceries on the way home? No. Get that long overdue haircut? Nah. Buy a nice present for your partner? Yes!

Beyond that you should do something nice for yourself. Not something that entails one of life's basic needs but something that you wouldn't otherwise buy because it is not normally affordable or a "good" expenditure of money. We are talking about wants here, not needs.

When I finally convinced my brother Tom that he not only deserved this but that it would induce and cultivate future winnings, a switch was flicked. He took a decent day's profit and bought himself a remote starter for his car. Other than summer/racing season it is pretty cold in his town, Saratoga, so it sure is nice to go out to a toasty car! Feels like more luxury than it is!

I had a friend who loved to play casino slots. Fred was the first person to put me on to this notion that winnings should be spent on wants, not needs. Fred was an over-the-top hedonistic and a lusty 450 pound man. His play was big too, though his bankroll was not. He would go in with $500 (not very much for craps) and either lose it all in a short span or win tons. He would toss the dice ten or more feet in the air and still hit the back wall! The pit boss didn't know what to do with him since technically he was doing nothing that violated the rules of the game. Nonetheless, they figured out some reason to tell him to stop or else they would throw him out and ban him from the casino for life! Fred responded by developing a new style of throwing the "bones". He would power toss them such that they hit the back wall and fly all over, knocking over stakes of chips and ricocheting off side walls like pinballs, eventually landing right back in front of him on the pass line.

One time, after we won big and played through the night, he stopped halfway home saying he needed to rest as he was so tired he was seeing peacocks crossing the highway! Upon awakening he got out of the car and promptly walked into the oriental rug shop that stood facing us. In a few minutes he returned with two men carrying a Turkish rug. Being a sensory slut, Fred wanted to feel the texture of that rug beneath his feet on a daily basis. Myself, when I got home I ordered a few very nice pens that I had been eyeing for a while.

After another marathon winning night, Fred once again pulled over to nap. Again, upon awakening, he walked into the store in front of him. A Cadillac dealership! He came out empty handed but told me we had to empty out the car. Then sure enough, up pulls the salesman with an old but low mile Caddie about the size of an Airstream travel trailer. We transferred our possessions and drove off in what Fred had bought with his trade in plus winnings. Fred lived large and driving large was a part of that. Myself, when I got home I bought myself a nicer watch that I had been eyeing for a while.

The moral of the tales is that for gambling to mean anything to you, you need to take all winnings and buy something you otherwise wouldn't. To do otherwise would rob yourself of the opportunity to enjoy yourself and the chance to teach your subconscious mind that "THIS IS WHAT I WANT MORE OF!"

Chapter Seventeen

Betting With
The Better Bettor

O n a cold dark winter night, I stood out by the paddock watching the horses walk the grooms around in circles before being saddled. It was the fifth race at Penn National. Three thousand dollar claimers seeking to win a six furlong crawl. If hell is in fact not burning hot but is instead frigidly cold as Dante once suggested, I was a tourist there minus a Virgil.

I liked the five horse, Kinky Boots. I set out for the nearest betting window, which happened to be outside and right off to the side of the paddock. Ahead of me in line was a groom. After he left, tickets in hand, I stepped up and asked what he bet and how much. Since HIPPA laws don't cover the confidentiality of a pari mutuel wager, the teller told me what I wanted to know. I said "give me the same thing". So I walked away having not bet Kinky but instead Norse the Horse to win for $100. I liked this tactic a lot since I figured that this was a great deal of money for a groom getting paid minimum wage or less. He obviously had inside information.

Norse won by 10 lengths having run like he never had before in his eight years on the track, paying $7.20. This was before simulcasting so I figured it was the grooms and my bet that had actually moved the board. 9-2 had dropped to 5-2, no doubt because the ten other people in attendance on that frozen night had their money on other choices.

In a similar vein, bet with those that win regularly. Likewise, avoid betting with those that lose most of the time. Regarding this latter point, a number of years ago I was watching one of the early cable programs that featured races from all over, four at a time, each in its own quadrant of the flatscreen. There were three color commentators. One was a former jockey, another a former trainer, and the third a one time track announcer. It was December 31st and they were comparing how they had fared playing the ponies in the last year.

It is good for your wallet to synch your psyche up with those that win, no matter if grooms or gazillionaires. Model what they do and how they do it.

It is also good to synch up with those that create the winners. For example, I had a friend who knew the track supervisor at a medium sized track. Each race day he would call to find out how the track would play. Was it tilled to favor closers or front running speed? Which lane was fastest, 1,3, 5?

Chapter Eighteen

Psychology and
The Betting Environment

You need to bet in a place where you feel good, positive, and gently optimistic. I am not getting all New Agey on you and talking "Feng Shui For Gamblers". We are talking about the basics. A pleasant environment, however you define that.

Does this mean that you visit Aqueduct on a dreary and frigid February? Nope. If you have ever been there you know that you are actually visiting one ring of handicapper hell. If you stay for the day's last race you are guaranteed to leave, with the ten others in attendance, deeply depressed and suicidal.

How about your study next to the mess of work that is still as yet undone? In eyesight of the five loads of dirty laundry waiting to be washed. Gazing out over that stack of dirty dishes beginning to smell in the sink?. No, not that.

A better alternative? Well, as I write this I sit in a comfy lounge chair in a nicely decorated study. Music plays softly in the background. Reno, my Rottweiler, rests by my side ready to attack and devour any false favourites that dare to appear on today's Santa Anita card. After every page of this book that I write I reward myself by handicapping a race. This works for me. Find your place of relaxed pleasant positivity.

Chapter Nineteen

The Finish Line

Having read this book and applied the tips spoken about you have learned and begun implementing:

- Sets of mental tools that will improve your handicapping.

- A previously secret and unspoken system that can be integrated with your current handicapping methods.

- Powerful cognitive techniques taught by the only Dr. of psychology to ever reveal how science can benefit you, the horse player.

- Highly refined observational skills developed from a deep and detailed understanding of owner, trainer, and horse behaviour.

To further own and integrate into your handicapping toolbox that which you have been taught, I recommend using the blank pages in this book to make a succinct list of the tips contained in each chapter. Review this "cheat sheet" regularly to ensure you are using all the handicapping weapons at your disposal!

Prior to doing that however, I advise you to use a different blank page to make a list of your handicapping strengths and weaknesses. The latter is particularly important because it will enable you to use the angles spoken of in this book in a highly targeted way.

Enjoy! Have fun! Win!

9 781735 480268